THE OREGON TRAIL

A TRUE BOOK®

by

Elaine Landau

Children's Press
A Division of Scholastic Inc.

New York Toronto London Auckland Sydney
Mexico City New Delhi Hong Kong
Danbury, Connecticut

A statue of a pioneer mother at the National Frontier Trails Museum in Missouri

Content Consultant
Jim Tompkins
Oregon Trail Historian, Author, and Educator

Reading Consultant
Dr. Cecilia Minden-Cupp
Former Director, Language and Literacy Program Harvard Graduate School of Education

Author's Dedication
For Hailey Louise Albers

The illustration on the cover shows pioneers traveling west in a covered wagon. The photograph on the title page shows a restored covered wagon on the Oregon Trail near Scotts Bluff, Nebraska.

Library of Congress Cataloging-in-Publication Data
Landau, Elaine.
    The Oregon Trail / by Elaine Landau.
        p. cm. — (A true book)
    Includes bibliographical references and index.
    ISBN 0-516-25871-0 (lib. bdg.)   0-516-27903-3 (pbk.)
    1. Pioneers—Oregon National Historic Trail—History—19th century—Juvenile literature. 2. Pioneers—Oregon National Historic Trail—Social life and customs—19th century—Juvenile literature. 3. Frontier and pioneer life—Oregon National Historic Trail—Juvenile literature. 4. Overland journeys to the Pacific—Juvenile literature. 5. Oregon National Historic Trail—History—Juvenile literature. I. Title. II. Series.
F597.L26 2006
978'.02—dc22   2005003639

CHILDREN'S PRESS, and A TRUE BOOK™, and associated logos are trademarks and/or registered trademarks of Scholastic Library Publishing. SCHOLASTIC and associated logos are trademarks and/or registered trademarks of Scholastic Inc.
1 2 3 4 5 6 7 8 9 10 R 15 14 13 12 11 10 09 08 07 06

Contents

Fur trappers set up early settlements in the Oregon Country.

Westward Bound

The year 1843 was an exciting time in the history of the United States. The nation was still growing. Everyone had heard stories about the unsettled West. Explorers and fur trappers spoke of a wonderful place. It had rich farmland and thick forests. It was the Oregon Country.

Some thought of the West as a place of freedom, open land, and endless opportunity. They believed that a hardworking family could leave tough times behind and build a better life there.

Many Americans dreamed of packing up and heading out to this land of promise. Actually getting to the Oregon Country was not easy, however. Settlers had to take the Oregon Trail. This **route** was about

The Oregon Country offered open land with great promise.

A map of the first Oregon Trail route

2,000 miles (3,218 kilometers) long. It went through what are now the states of Missouri, Kansas, Nebraska, Wyoming, Idaho, and Oregon.

The Oregon Trail wound its way across prairies, deserts, rivers, and mountain passes. It was rugged and often dangerous territory. There were many dangers along the way. Not everyone who started the journey finished it. One in ten **pioneers** died on the trail.

Fear did not stop the first large group of settlers. They began the trip in 1843. There were about one hundred families. Their trip was known as the great **migration**, and the travelers were known as **emigrants**. It was the start of a westward movement that lasted for twenty-five years.

By the time it was over, as many as 500,000 people had journeyed to Oregon on the Oregon Trail. This important

In the great migration of 1843, a large group of settlers headed to Oregon.

route opened up Oregon as well as the territories of Washington, California, Nevada, Idaho, and Utah to other settlers and development.

The Way to Statehood

A map of the Oregon Country

President James K. Polk

Before 1846, what is now roughly America's Pacific Northwest was called the Oregon Country. In 1848, President James K. Polk signed a bill creating the Oregon Territory, which included part of the Oregon Country. Oregon did not become a U.S. state until 1859.

Pulling Up Stakes

Families moved west in covered wagons. The trip was far too difficult and dangerous for families to set off on their own. They usually traveled in groups of wagons called **wagon trains.** As many as one hundred wagons would travel together.

In the early years, the starting point for people traveling the

Emigrants moved west in groups called wagon trains.

Oregon Trail was Independence, Missouri, near the Missouri River. Families gathered there

Sample supplies for the Oregon Trail are displayed at the National Frontier Trails Museum.

with their wagons packed tightly with supplies. The settlers brought flour, sugar, rice, beans, bacon, dried fruit, and coffee beans for the journey. They also took pots, pans, and kettles to cook with.

Every family had a rifle, axe, shovel, and other tools necessary to clear the land for farming after they arrived. Many settlers brought the farm animals they would need when they reached Oregon. The oxen used to pull their wagons would later pull their farm plows. They took cows, mules, hogs, and chickens, too.

Wagons Ho!

A day on the Oregon Trail began before dawn. Each morning, men on horseback fired shots in the air as a wake-up call. The women rose and lit cooking fires to start breakfast. There was no time to waste. The settlers had to eat their **griddlecakes** and

bacon quickly before hitching
up their wagons.

Before long, the wagons took
their place in line. By sunup,
they were rolling westward.

The end of this wagon train moves slowly over a mountain.

A wagon's place in the wagon train was extremely important. It was best to be in front. Wagons in the rear had to ride through the dust kicked up by those ahead of them. In some wagon trains, people took turns being in front. That saved some families from being covered with dust during the entire trip. In other wagon trains, the most senior and respected families always drove in front.

Most settlers walked alongside the wagons. Wagons were almost always pulled by oxen and mules, not horses.

Every family had one or two wagons. Some families could afford to have three or more wagons. People usually walked alongside the wagons most of the way to Oregon. This lightened the load for the animals pulling the wagons. These animals had to be preserved for future challenges, such as getting over the mountains.

There was little free time on a wagon train. Settlers started out in the late spring. They had to reach Oregon before the winter set in. It was best to complete the journey in no more than five months. Any longer and a wagon train might find itself in serious trouble. Once the heavy snows began, a wagon train could not make it through the mountains.

Some days, the settlers were able to cover 20 miles (32 km), but many days they went fewer. Using oxen to pull the wagons sometimes slowed the trip, especially if the trail was steep. The wagons stopped

Wagon travel in the winter was dangerous and slow.

briefly for lunch each day. Sometimes settlers just ate dried meat before hurrying on.

The wagon train did not stop again until it was almost dark.

Then the settlers put their wagons in a circle and lit their campfires. They unhitched and fed their animals before eating their own dinner. Usually they ate what they brought with them, until it ran out.

Buffalo Chips

Finding enough wood to keep the campfires burning was a common problem.

Cooking on a fire fueled with buffalo chips

Along parts of the trail, there were few trees. So the settlers used dried pieces of buffalo droppings instead of wood as fuel. Settlers soon learned that the larger dried buffalo droppings burned best. Collecting the buffalo chips was like picking up firewood. When they were burned for heat or for cooking, they produced an odorless fire.

On the trail, the settlers hunted buffalo when they could.

When traveling on the Great Plains, the settlers might have buffalo or antelope for dinner. During other parts of the trip, fresh meat was far scarcer. At times, they only had dry bread and bacon for breakfast, lunch, and dinner.

After dinner, the settlers did any necessary repairs on the wagons. There might be a little time left to relax. Families shared stories around the campfires. Some evenings, the sound of someone playing a fiddle or harmonica filled the night air. Children practiced their lessons. Some people had prayer meetings. Many groups sang songs, while others danced.

Then the campfires were put out. The tired settlers were anxious to go to sleep. Before long, they would awaken to the sound of gun-fire and the start of another day of travel.

A fiddler provides music for tired travelers by the campfire.

Dangers of the Trail

Traveling on the Oregon Trail could be dangerous. Many settlers feared attacks from American Indians. Yet the Indians were usually helpful. At times, they pulled the settlers' wagons out of the mud. They also guided the wagon trains across rivers and steep

American Indians helped the white settlers on the Oregon Trail in many ways.

mountain passes. Indians also approached the wagon trains to trade horses and food for clothing, guns, and tobacco.

The Indians may not have been a great threat on the Oregon Trail, but there were other dangers. Many settlers were killed or injured in accidents. Because people were sometimes careless while cleaning or carrying their rifles, a few settlers died from accidental gunshot wounds. In other cases, children who fell along the way were crushed beneath a wagon's heavy wheels.

A hand holds a pioneer child's wooden buttons above his grave marker, dug up by a farmer in the 1960s. Joel Hembree died on the Oregon Trail after being struck by a wagon in 1843.

A pioneer family struggles during a prairie windstorm.

Terrible storms on the prairie took their toll, too. Some settlers were struck and killed by lightning. Many more lives were lost during the dangerous river crossings along the trail. Some of the rivers were deeper and more powerful than the settlers realized. Hundreds drowned trying to make their way across.

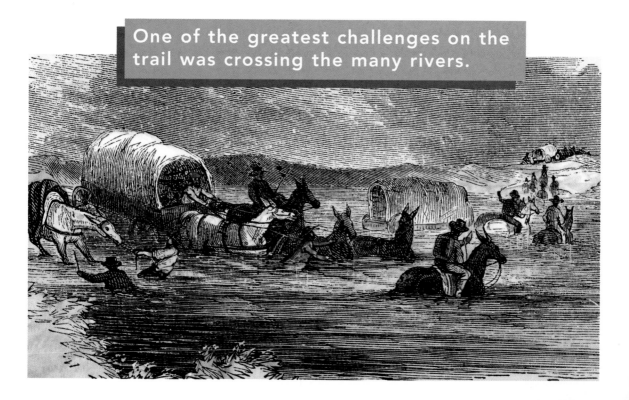

One of the greatest challenges on the trail was crossing the many rivers.

Animals were another danger of the trail. Some pioneers died when buffalo charged the wagon trains, oxen bolted, or horses threw riders. Rattlesnakes were the most deadly wild animals for the settlers.

However, the biggest killer on the Oregon Trail was disease. **Cholera,** an often deadly disease of the intestines, spread easily from one person to another. Victims often became extremely ill and died within twenty-four

This wagon-wheel rim marks the grave of Rebecca Winters, who died of cholera along the trail.

hours. So many deaths on the trail meant that often there was time only for a simple burial before moving on.

Arrival

After arriving in the Oregon Country, most of the early families settled in the Willamette Valley near Oregon City. Despite the hardships along the trail, the settlers were usually glad they came. Families cleared the land to build homes and plant crops. The mild weather was perfect for

The Willamette Valley continues to have productive farmland.

farming. Oregon was also free of many of the diseases common in more settled areas back East. Many settlers raised their families in Oregon and came to think of it as their home.

The wagon trains kept coming regularly. Then in 1869, the **transcontinental railroad** linking the East to the West was finally completed. The railroad to California changed the style of travel. People going west began to take the train. But even after the railroad, wagon trains continued until about 1920.

The Oregon Trail has not been forgotten. It helped expand the country, making

These wagon ruts remain from Oregon Trail days.

those who traveled it true pioneers. The Oregon Trail is an important part of U.S. history. Even today, this famous route draws regular visitors to its historic trail sites.

To Find Out More

Here are some additional resources to help you learn more about the Oregon Trail:

 **Books**

Kay, Verla. **Covered Wagons, Bumpy Trails.** Putnam, 2000.

Littlefield, Holly. **Children of the Trail West.** Carolrhoda, 1999.

Patent, Dorothy Hinshaw. **West by Covered Wagon: Retracing the Pioneer Trails.** Walker, 1995.

Quasha, Jennifer. **Covered Wagons: Hands-On Projects About America's Westward Expansion.** PowerKids Press, 2003.

Stanley, Diane. **Roughing It on the Oregon Trail.** HarperCollins, 1999.

Williams, David. **Grandma Essie's Covered Wagon.** Knopf, 1993.

Organizations and Online Sites

Museum of Westward Expansion

11 North Fourth Street
St. Louis, MO 63102
314-655-1700
http://www.nps.gov/jeff/ mus-tour.htm

Explore the world of the American Indians and the nineteenth-century pioneers who helped shape the history of the American West.

Oregon National Historic Trail

http://www.nps.gov/oreg/ oreg/history.htm

Read about the history of the Oregon Trail. Learn details about visiting sites on the historic trail.

National Frontier Trails Museum

318 West Pacific Avenue
Independence, MO 64050
816-325-7575
http://www.frontiertrailscenter. com

Check out this museum and its site, dedicated to the history of America's main western trails.

End of the Oregon Trail Interpretive Center

1726 Washington Street
Oregon City, OR 97045
503-657-9336
http://www.endofthe oregontrail.org

Visit this hands-on museum and its informative site to find out more about the Oregon Trail and the early period of Northwest settlement.

Important Words

cholera an often deadly disease of the intestines

emigrants people who leave a region to live in another region

griddlecakes flat cakes of thin batter fried on both sides on a griddle

migration movement from one country or region to another

pioneers people who explore and settle an unknown area, such as the Oregon Country

route a road or trail followed to get from one place to another

transcontinental railroad a railroad that runs across a continent

wagon trains large groups of covered wagons traveling together

Index

Meet the Author

Award-winning author Elaine Landau worked as a newspaper reporter, an editor, and a youth-services librarian before becoming a full-time writer. She has written more than 250 nonfiction books for young people, including True Books on dinosaurs, animals, countries, and food. Ms. Landau has a bachelor's degree in English and journalism from New York University as well as a master's degree in library and information science. She lives with her husband and son in Miami, Florida.

Photographs © 2006: Brown Brothers: 4, 15, 20; Corbis Images: 12, 27, 35 (James L. Amos), 22 (Bettmann), 41 (Bohemian Nomad Picturemakers), 13 bottom (The Corcoran Gallery of Art), 16 (Richard Cummings), 28 (Leonard de Selva), 39 (Lowell Georgia), 2 (Connie Ricca), 13 top; Denver Public Library, Western History Collection: 11 (by William Henry Jackson, WHJ-10613); North Wind Picture Archives: 1 (Nancy Carter), cover, 7, 25, 31, 33, 36, 37, 43; Superstock, Inc.: 26 (Huntington Library, San Marino, CA), 19.

Map by Bob Italiano